anything.

Math

in Science

Thanks to the creative team:
Senior Editor: Alice Peebles
Illustration: Dan Newman
Fact checking: Tom Jackson
Picture Research: Nic Dean
Design: Perfect Bound Ltd

Hungry Tomato®
A division of Lerner Publishing Group, Inc.
241 First Avenue North
Minneapolis, MN 55401 USA

For reading levels and more information, look up this title at www.lernerbooks.com.

Main body text set in Panton Regular 10.5/13.

Library of Congress Cataloging-in-Publication Data

Names: Dickmann, Nancy, author.
Title: Math in science / Nancy Dickmann.
Description: Minnespolis : Hungry Tomato, [2018] | Series: The amazing world of math | Audience: Ages 8–12. | Audience: Grades 4 to 6.
Identifiers: LCCN 2017060520 (print) | LCCN 2017056682 (ebook) | ISBN 9781541523906 (eb pdf) | ISBN 9781541500983 (lb : alk. paper)
Subjects: LCSH: Science—Mathematics—Juvenile literature. | Mathematics—Juvenile literature.
Classification: LCC Q175.32.M38 (print) | LCC Q175.32.M38 D53 2018 (ebook) | DDC 501/.51—dc23

LC record available at https://lccn.loc.gov/2017060520

Manufactured in the United States of America
1-43767-33627-2/2/2018

The Amazing World of Math

Math
in Science

Nancy Dickmann

HUNGRY TOMATO®

Minneapolis

Contents

Math
All around Us

People have been studying math for thousands of years. In fact, many of the world's most important inventions and scientific discoveries are based in math!

*Math helps fighter jets **navigate** with pinpoint accuracy, even in the dark of night.*

Discovering the World

Did you know that people once thought the sun traveled around Earth? Or that scientists were able to predict new chemical **elements** by sorting them into groups? Over the centuries, we have vastly increased our knowledge of the world around us—and many of these discoveries were made using math. In fact, the ancient Greek mathematician Pythagoras once said that "all is number." He was probably right!

The ancient Romans were brilliant **engineers**, using math to design structures so tough they are still standing today. This Roman aqueduct is the Pont du Gard in the South of France (see pages 10–11).

Measuring the Earth

Long before satellites were invented, a Greek mathematician called Eratosthenes estimated the **circumference** of Earth. His answer was surprisingly accurate!

A Round World

Eratosthenes lived in Alexandria, Egypt, an important center of Greek culture. Back then, scientists already knew that Earth was spherical (ball-shaped), but no one knew exactly how big it was. Eratosthenes decided to work it out using **geometry**.

Eratosthenes used math to map much of the known world.

SUN'S RAYS

Math in Action!

The distance between Alexandria and Syene is about 500 miles (800 km). If that is $7/360$ of Earth's circumference, what is Earth's circumference? Use a calculator to work it out.

This is how Eratosthenes worked out Earth's circumference.

Angled Light

Eratosthenes knew that at noon on the first day of summer in the town of Syene, the sun was directly overhead. However, at the same time in Alexandria, it was not. A stick in Syene would cast no shadow, while a stick in Alexandria would. This was because the sun's rays were hitting the two cities at different **angles**. The difference in angle proved that Earth's surface is curved.

In Alexandria, the angle from the top of a stick to the end of the shadow it cast was about 7 **degrees** (written as 7°). There are 360° in a circle, so Eratosthenes **estimated** that the distance from Alexandria to Syene was $^{7}/_{360}$ of Earth's circumference. He knew the distance between the two cities, so he used math to work out what the entire circumference would be.

In Syene, when the sun was directly overhead, its reflection could be seen at the bottom of a deep well.

7°

Alexandria

Well at
Syene

7°

Amazing Arches

There are many ancient structures still standing today. A lot of them have one shape in common—the amazing arch.

A vaulted ceiling is made from interlocking arch shapes.

The arches in this aqueduct supported the channel on top that carried water to cities.

Flat Lintels

Before arches, gaps in a structure (such as a doorway or the span of a bridge) were made by resting a flat beam called a lintel across two posts. The problem with this system was that the gaps couldn't be very big. A long stone lintel would be very heavy, and it couldn't support large loads.

Here Come the Romans

The ancient Romans were masters of the stone arch. These shapes could span bigger gaps. An arch is made of smaller wedge-shaped blocks. The blocks are easy to carry and work with, and they fit together to form a semicircle. The arch sits atop two columns. The weight of the load that the arch carries is transferred down its columns.

Although wide arches could carry heavy loads, their columns had to be big and strong. The Romans discovered that you could use thinner columns if you built many arches in a row. The arches helped to support each other. These rows were used in the aqueducts that brought water to Rome.

The semicircular dome is another very strong shape used by Roman builders. It is made of arches arranged in a circle.

Math in Action!

You need to build a stone arch bridge over a river. The river is 100 yards wide. Your design uses arches that are 5 yards wide. How many arches will you need to cross the river?

Keeping Time

We divide time into minutes, hours, and days. But before clocks were invented, measuring time wasn't easy.

Tracking the Sun

Long ago, there was no universal system for measuring time. People divided the day or night into different units, but the units varied from place to place. Sometimes they even changed length! The ancient Egyptians divided the time between sunrise and sunset into 12 hours. Days are longer in summer, so summer hours were longer than winter hours.

The **sundial** was an early device for measuring time. The sun moves across the sky throughout the day, making shadows change shape. A sundial has a pointer called a gnomon, which casts a shadow. The shadow falls on a dial that has the hours marked. As the sun moves, the gnomon's shadow does too.

Each sundial was designed for a particular location. It wouldn't work properly if it was moved elsewhere.

Water and Wheels

Another type of clock used water. Water would flow at a steady rate from one container to another. Marks on the container showed how much time had passed. In about 1300, mechanical clocks began to appear. These used weights pulling on an arrangement of gears and wheels. The earliest versions had no faces or hands—they only struck the hours.

In some water clocks, the rising water level moved a dial.

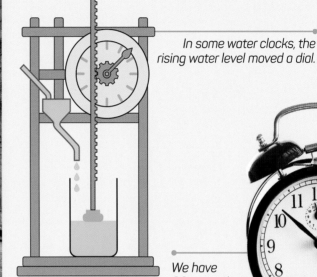

This clock in Prague has been tracking the sun's movements since 1410.

We have 60 seconds in a minute and 60 minutes in an hour thanks to a system devised by the ancient Babylonians. Their counting system used 60 as a base, instead of 100. Sixty is more useful because it can be divided by many more numbers than 100 can.

Math in Action!

There are 60 minutes in an hour and 24 hours in a day. Can you work out how many minutes there are in a week? Use a calculator if you need to.

Circling the Sun

As we stand on Earth's surface, it doesn't feel as if it's moving. For a long time, people assumed that it didn't. It took some clever math to work out the truth.

Center of the Universe

Ancient people watched how the sun, moon, stars, and **planets** moved. They knew that different objects moved in different ways. As everything they could see appeared to move, and Earth felt solid, they decided that all the objects in the sky traveled around Earth.

*The planets **orbit** at different distances from the sun.*

Wait a Minute...

The problem was that some planets appeared to move backward at certain times. An astronomer called Ptolemy worked out a complicated system to explain this. It involved planets making loops like a roller coaster in their orbits.

In the 1500s, a Polish mathematician, Nicolaus Copernicus, began crunching numbers. He analyzed data on the positions of stars and planets, looking for a way to explain their movement. He concluded that all the planets—including Earth—travel around the sun in circular paths.

Once **telescopes** were invented, **astronomers** used them to find evidence that Copernicus had been right.

Copernicus's ideas were published just before he died. They caused a lot of arguments.

Math in Action!

Johannes Kepler later discovered that the planets' orbits are actually **ellipses**, not circles. Draw your own ellipse by using thumbtacks to fasten a piece of string over a piece of paper. (There should be some slack in the string.) Put the tip of a pencil against the string and pull it taut. Move the pencil in an arc, keeping the string taut, until you have completed an ellipse.

Seeing Farther

The astronomers who proved Copernicus's ideas had a powerful tool: the telescope. It made use of **lenses** and angles.

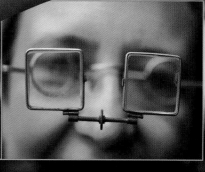

Very early magnifying glasses like these helped surgeons see when operating.

When we look through a lens, objects appear bigger or smaller than they actually are—and sometimes upside down!

Rays of Light

We see objects because of rays of light that travel in straight lines into our eyes. A lens is a curved piece of glass, plastic, or crystal. Light can travel through these materials, but their shape bends the light rays and makes them change direction. This makes the rays appear to come from somewhere closer or farther away.

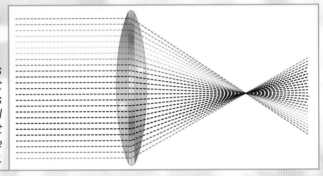

A lens bends light by different amounts along its curved surface. All the beams meet at a place called the focal point.

Using Lenses

Simple lenses were used in ancient times, probably to start fires. Focusing the sun's rays on a small area makes it heat up and catch fire. Scribes and craftworkers may have used lenses to see small things more clearly.

People got better at making lenses. They adjusted the curve of the lens to bend light rays at exactly the angle they wanted. In the 1280s, eyeglasses were invented. In the late 1500s, lens makers learned to use more than one lens to increase magnifying power. They began making **microscopes** and telescopes.

The Italian astronomer Galileo was one of the first people to use lenses to look at the sky.

Math in Action!

Water bends light, just as glass can. A drop of water has a curved surface that works like a lens. Take an old newspaper and lay a piece of clear plastic wrap over it. Carefully place a single drop of water on the plastic and look at the type below. It should be magnified by your water lens.

Tough Triangles

Arches are strong, but another shape dominates construction today. Engineers use triangles in bridges, buildings and other structures.

Polygons

Any shape with straight sides is called a polygon. Triangles are polygons and so are squares and hexagons. A triangle has three sides, which join at three angles. The sides do not all have to be the same length, and the angles can be different too.

This skyscraper's frame has triangular braces for extra support.

Can you see the triangles in this steel bridge?

Strong and Rigid

A square has four sides and four angles. In a square shape, the angles can act a bit like hinges. If you squash a square, the angles change to form a shape called a rhombus (below). But a triangle doesn't do this. It can't twist or change its angles unless the lengths of its sides change.

Structures that are built of steel beams often fix the beams in triangle shapes for strength. If squares are used, another beam is often placed diagonally across the square. This beam divides the square into two triangles and provides extra stability.

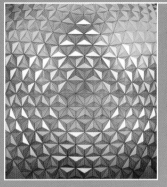

The dome of the Epcot Center at Walt Disney World Resort, Florida, gets its strength from hundreds of triangles.

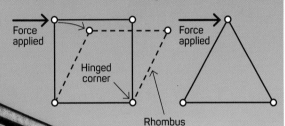

Force applied

Hinged corner

Rhombus

Force applied

Math in Action!

Cut out strips of card of equal lengths. Punch a hole at both ends of each strip. Use brass paper fasteners to connect the strips to form shapes, such as a triangle, square, and hexagon. Hold your shapes by opposite corners and move them back and forth to test how rigid they are. How do they compare?

Ones and Zeros

1 is 1, but can 10 be 1010? Thanks to a number system developed by Gottfried Leibniz, it can— and that's how we came to have computers!

Leibniz developed his ideas in the 1670s.

DANGER

DANGER

All about That Base

Our number system is called Base 10, or decimal. Each digit in a number represents a place value, and the different place values go up in multiples of ten: ones, tens, hundreds, thousands. Leibniz's system was called Base 2, or binary. The place values go up in multiples of two: ones, twos, fours, eights, and so on.

In a **binary number**, the only digits allowed are 0 and 1. You can see how it works here:

Decimal number	Eights column	Fours column	Twos column	Ones column	Binary number	How it works
3			1	1	11	2+1 = 3
5		1	0	1	101	4+0+1 = 5
10	1	0	1	0	1010	8+0+2+0 = 10
15	1	1	1	1	1111	8+4+2+1 = 15

The binary system made modern electronic computers possible. Computer memory is made up of small elements or switches that can be either off or on. We use 1 to tell the switch to be on and 0 to tell it to be off. All **data** can be converted into binary.

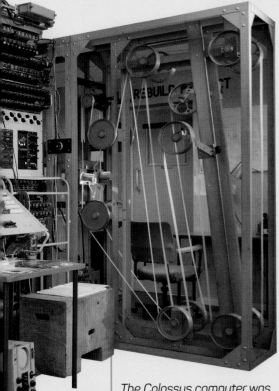

The Colossus computer was built during World War II to help crack secret codes.

In World War II, the work of code-breaking mathematicians helped ships avoid submarines and saved thousands of lives.

Math in Action!

Make your own binary table, using the one above as a model but adding a sixteens column and a thirty-twos column. Can you translate the following decimal numbers into binary?

7 = _____

14 = _____

25 = _____

40 = _____

21

The Metric Revolution

We all know how long a meter is, but how about a **stadion** or a **parasang**? And do you know how many **rods** make up a **league**?

The United States has not officially adopted the metric system. However, the influence of the metric system can be seen in many aspects of our lives, from the gym to the supermarket.

Different Systems

Long ago, there were many different systems of measurement. Some of them were based on the human body, such as the foot. But the foot in different cultures could be different lengths. Other units for measuring weight or volume were completely different from place to place. The result? A lot of confusion!

Going Metric

In 1670, a French mathematician suggested a new system for measuring length. The unit of measure would be based on the Earth's circumference and be divided up decimally (by tens). More than a century later, scientists measured a line of **longitude** and used it to decide on the length of the meter.

The meter is what's called a base unit, and **prefixes** were added for larger or smaller units. A *centi*meter is one-hundredth of a meter, and a *kilo*meter is 1,000 meters. Before long, the metric system was expanded to include **mass**, **volume,** and area. The units are linked. For example, one gram is equivalent to the mass of a cube of water with sides of 1 centimeter.

The Roman mile was a unit of measure based on how far a soldier could walk in 1,000 paces.

Thermometers may show the metric Celsius scale along with the older Fahrenheit scale.

Prefix	Meaning
kilo	1,000
hecto	100
deca	10
deci	0.1 or $^1/_{10}$
centi	0.01 or $^1/_{100}$
milli	0.001 or $^1/_{1000}$

Math in Action!

Use the table of metric prefixes to convert these metric measurements into other units.

1 liter = _____ deciliters

154 centimeters = _____ meters

3 kilograms = _____ grams

25 millimeters = _____ centimeters

It's Elementary!

The best way to make sense of data is to organize it in a logical way. A Russian chemist used a table to classify the chemical elements.

Elements

All matter is made up of substances called elements. There are more than 100 elements, all with different **properties**. Many are solid at room temperature, but some are liquid or gas.

Each square in the table represents an element and shows information about it.

Putting Things in Order

Nearly 200 years ago, one chemist tried to organize the elements in groups of three. He looked for patterns in the average weights of the elements, but they wouldn't all fit neatly into groups. In 1869, Dmitri Mendeleev published a new approach.

Mendeleev also organized the elements by weight, making a table in which mass increases as you read each row from left to right. He tried to arrange it so that elements with similar properties formed vertical columns. In some places this meant leaving gaps in the rows. Mendeleev assumed that new elements would eventually be found to fill the gaps in his periodic table, as it was called.

Dmitri Mendeleev was honored by having a new element named after him.

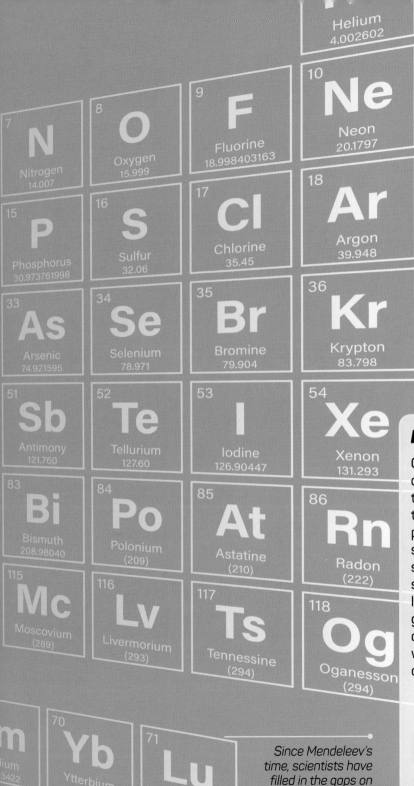

			Helium 4.002602
7 **N** Nitrogen 14.007	8 **O** Oxygen 15.999	9 **F** Fluorine 18.998403163	10 **Ne** Neon 20.1797
15 **P** Phosphorus 30.973761998	16 **S** Sulfur 32.06	17 **Cl** Chlorine 35.45	18 **Ar** Argon 39.948
33 **As** Arsenic 74.921595	34 **Se** Selenium 78.971	35 **Br** Bromine 79.904	36 **Kr** Krypton 83.798
51 **Sb** Antimony 121.760	52 **Te** Tellurium 127.60	53 **I** Iodine 126.90447	54 **Xe** Xenon 131.293
83 **Bi** Bismuth 208.98040	84 **Po** Polonium (209)	85 **At** Astatine (210)	86 **Rn** Radon (222)
115 **Mc** Moscovium (289)	116 **Lv** Livermorium (293)	117 **Ts** Tennessine (294)	118 **Og** Oganesson (294)

| ...lium ...3422 | 70 **Yb** Ytterbium 173.045 | 71 **Lu** Lutetium 174.9668 | |
| ...d | 102 **No** ...elevium | 103 ... | |

Copper, silver, and gold are all in the same vertical column, Group 11. They have similar properties.

Math in Action!

Collect a wide variety of candies and try to organize them into your own periodic table. You could look at properties such as size, shape, color, flavor, and so on. Can you work out a system to arrange them in logical periods (rows) and groups (columns)? You could also try this activity with socks, building blocks, or types of breakfast cereal.

Since Mendeleev's time, scientists have filled in the gaps on the periodic table.

Finding Our Way

We take satnav for granted, but do you know how it works? This amazing invention links **satellites** and math.

Around the World

Satnav is short for satellite navigationv. Most satnav devices use signals from a network of satellites called the Global Positioning System (GPS). There are more than 24 satellites in the network, orbiting high above Earth's surface.

Many GPS receivers have map programs to help you find your way.

No matter where you are, you will be in range of at least four GPS satellites.

Where Are You?

The satellites send out signals, which a GPS device receives. The device works out how long the signal takes to reach it, then calculates how far it is from the satellite. To tell you where you are, a device needs signals from three satellites at the same time.

If you are 100 miles (161 km) from Satellite 1, you could be anywhere on a sphere with the satellite at the center and a **radius** of 100 miles. If you are 90 miles (145 km) from Satellite 2, that makes another sphere, and if you are 110 miles (177 km) from Satellite 3, that makes a third. There will only be one point where all three spheres **intersect**. The GPS receiver does the math and tells you exactly where you are. This is called trilateration.

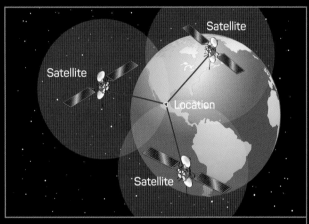

Satellite

Satellite

Location

Satellite

No matter where you are, it only takes three satellites to get a fix on your position.

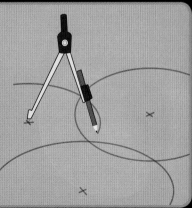

Math in Action!

Use a ruler and a pair of compasses to try trilateration. Mark three points on a piece of paper, roughly in a triangle arrangement. These are your "satellites." Use the ruler to measure out a distance from the first satellite, then draw a circle with the satellite at the center. Repeat for the other two satellites, using different distances. In how many places do the circles intersect?

Math in Action:
Answers & Tips

How did you do with the 10 math challenges? Here are the correct answers and some tips on how to work them out.

Page 9: Based on Eratosthenes' method and the measurements in the question, Earth's circumference is about 25,560 miles (41,040 km). You know that 500 miles (800 km) is $^7/_{360}$ of the total circumference, so you need to work out what $^{360}/_{360}$ would be. First, use a calculator to divide 500 by 7: 500 ÷ 7 = 71 (rounded down to the nearest whole number). This figure is $^1/_{360}$ of the circumference. To find the whole circumference, multiply it by 360: 71 x 360 = 25,560.

Since the time of Eratosthenes, we have been able to measure Earth's circumference much more accurately. It is 24,900 miles (40,030 km), so his estimate was impressively close!

Page 11: You need 20 arches to span the bridge. This is a simple division problem. The river is 100 yards wide, and the arches are each 5 yards wide. To work out how many 5-yard arches will fit in 100 yards, divide: 100 ÷ 5 = 20.

To make it easier to work it out in your head, you can use place value, as follows.

Knock one of the 0s off the 100 to make 10. Now you have an easier division problem: 10 ÷ 5 = 2. Add the 0 back onto the result to get 20.

Page 13: There are 10,080 minutes in a week. First you need to work out how many minutes there are in a day. Do this by multiplying (with a calculator to help if you need): 60 x 24 = 1,440. Now you multiply that number by 7 (the number of days in a week) to get the final answer: 1,440 x 7 = 10,080.

Page 15: Did your shape look more or less oval? A string with a lot of slack will produce an ellipse that is closer in shape to a circle. A string with less slack will give you a wider, shorter ellipse.

To stop the string and pencil getting tangled up in the thumbtacks, you may need to lift up the pencil and re-set it once or twice.

Page 17: Did the water lens work to magnify the type? You may need to slightly adjust the angle from which you look at it. Has it distorted the type as well as magnifying it?

Target number	32	16	8	4	2	1	Answer
7				1	1	1	**111** (4 + 2 + 1 = 7)
14			1	1	1	0	**1110** (8 + 4 + 2 + 0 = 14)
25		1	1	0	0	1	**11001** (16 + 8 + 0 + 0 + 1 = 25)
40	1	0	1	0	0	0	**101000** (32 + 0 + 8 + 0 + 0 + 0 = 40)

For the math challenge on page 21.

Page 19: A triangle shape shouldn't move at all. The angles in a triangle can't change unless the lengths of the sides change too. The sides in your model stay the same length, so the angles won't be able to move.

A square shape can be easily changed into a rhombus. A hexagon can go into a number of different shapes—including a rectangle!

Page 21: Follow the table at the top of this page to work out the numbers in binary.

Page 23: 1 liter = 10 deciliters. Deci means 0.1 or $1/10$. If a deciliter is $1/10$ of a liter, then there must be 10 of them in a liter.

154 centimeters = 1.54 meters. Centi means 0.01 or $1/100$. This means that there are 100 centimeters in a meter, so 154 centimeters must be 1.54 meters.

3 kilograms = 3,000 grams. Kilo means 1,000, so there are 1,000 grams in a kilogram. To find out how many grams in 3 kilograms, just multiply: 3 x 1,000 = 3,000.

25 millimeters = 2.5 centimeters. This one is a little bit trickier. Milli means 0.001 or $1/1000$, so there are 1,000 millimeters in a meter. You've already worked out that there are 100 centimeters in a meter. This means that 100 centimeters = 1,000 millimeters. 100 x 10 = 1,000, so there must be 10 millimeters in a centimeter. 25 millimeters would be 2.5 centimeters.

Page 25: There is no right or wrong answer to this activity, and you may end up with gaps or items that don't quite seem to fit. Say that you chose to sort candies. Start by laying them out in a long row, from smallest to largest.

Now try to break up that row into a few shorter segments of equal length that can sit one on top of another, like the rows in the periodic table. Can you arrange them so that candies that fall in the same column have similar properties?

You could try to end up with columns that are all the same color, or all the same shape. You can adjust your rows by leaving gaps if it helps the candies to line up in a more logical way.

Page 27: If you've drawn your circles correctly, there should only be one place where all three circles meet. If the circles aren't all touching, you may have made one or two of the circles too small.

Glossary

angle: the space between two lines that come from a central point. Angles are measured in degrees.

astronomer: person who studies the sun, planets, and other objects in space

binary number: number made up of 1s and 0s which has place values representing 1, 2, 4, 8, 16 and so on

circumference: length of the line that forms the outside edge of a circle

data: information in the form of text, images, and sound that is stored and transmitted by computer

degree: unit for measuring angles, with the symbol °

element: substance that cannot be broken down or separated into other substances

ellipse: oval shape that looks like a flattened circle

engineer: person who uses science to design and build structures, machines, or new products

estimate: to make a careful guess about something

geometry: the study of shapes and angles

intersect: to meet or cross at a point

league: early, variable unit of distance traveled in an hour: about 3 miles (5 km)

lens: curved piece of clear material that bends the light rays passing through it

longitude: distance east or west on Earth's surface, measured in degrees

mass: the total amount of matter in an object or space

microscope: tool used for studying small objects, which makes them appear bigger

navigate: to find one's way

orbit: the path an object takes around a larger object; or, to take such a path

parasang: unit of length in ancient Persia, equivalent to the league

planet: large, spherical object that orbits the sun or another star

prefix: a word part with its own meaning added to the beginning of a word to make a new word with a different meaning

property: quality or characteristic, such as strength or hardness

radius: the distance from the center of a circle or sphere to its edge

rod: old measure of land length especially, equal to about 5 $\frac{1}{2}$ yards (5 m)

satellite: something that orbits a planet or other object in space

sundial: a device that uses a shadow cast by the sun to show the time of day

stadion: ancient Greek unit of measurement, about the length of a sports stadium of the time

telescope: tool used for studying space, which gathers information about things that are far away

volume: the total amount of space inside a three-dimensional shape

Amazing Math Facts

The famous Colosseum in Rome has an outer wall made mainly of arches. The lower three stories are rings of 80 arches each. They support a massive weight.

Near the equator, shadows cast by the sun are shorter than the shadows in places closer to the poles. A sundial made for use near the equator would not work if it was moved a long way north or south.

Two French surveyors spent six years measuring the distances along Earth's surface that would form the basis of the meter. Once the length of the meter was finalized, a platinum bar of the exact length was placed in France's National Archives as a reference.

The largest optical lenses ever used in a telescope measured 4 feet (1.25 m) across. The two lenses were set in a steel tube that was 65 yards (60 m) long. It could magnify objects to more than 500 times.

Copernicus was not the first person to suggest that Earth travelled around the sun. A Greek mathematician called Aristarchus proposed this more than 2,200 years ago.

Index

The Author

Nancy Dickmann worked in publishing for many years before becoming a full-time author. Now, with Pushkin the Three-Legged Wonder Cat as her trusty assistant (in charge of lap-sitting), she writes books on a wide range of topics, including animals, space, history, health, and explorers. The highlight of her career so far has been getting to interview a real astronaut to find out how they use the toilet in space!

Picture credits

(abbreviations· t = top; b = bottom; c = centre;
l = left; r = right)
Alamy Stock Photo: ART Collection 8 & 28; Photo 12 15;
Mike Stone 20; Malcolm Park editorial 16br; ITAR-TASS
Photo Agency 24; Derrick Alderman 4 & 16.
Dan Newman: 13c, 17tr & br, 19br, 25cr, 27br & 28br.
Shutterstock.com: 5 second Studio 25br & 29cr;
Alexander A. Nedviga 24t; Amzhylttay 31br; Andrey
Armyagov 2; ; Belenos 31tl; Bertl123 7tr & 10; Bildagentur
Zoonar GmbH 10tr; Chunni4691 23c; Dominik Michalek 12;
duntaro 24; ffly 6; ffly 6; Foto-Ruhrgebiet 25cr; Gervasio
S. _ Eureka_89 26bl; Harvepino 8; Horth Rasur 13; Inked
Pixels 9tr; iryna1 17bl; Istimages 31cl; Ivan Cholakov 1; JRP
Studio 3, 13cr & 28tr; kikujungboy 22; Kunal Mehta 18tr;
maskalin 21cr; Naeblys 14; Neil Wigmore 12; Nicku 20tr;
Pavel Ilyukhin 11tl; Philip Bird LRPS CPAGB 32; Richard
A McMillin 18; Robert Noel de Tilly 19tr; Roy Palmer 25tr;
trabantos 15tr; Vuk Kostic 23t; Zverge 25cr.
Wikimedia Commons: 26, 31tr & bl.